Goal Sett

Steps To Keep Motivated
& Master Your Personal
Goals

Matt Morris, CPCC

Table of Contents

Introduction

You're here because you want to achieve something. You have a goal. So what is it? Is it to get out of bed today and feel excited about your day? Maybe it's to write a book that you've been putting off for way too long? Spend more time with your family? Rekindle lost relationships? Maybe run a half-marathon by the end of the year? Or drop 15 pounds? Or travel to Europe or Australia? Or maybe start a business that you love and are passionate about? Or get into an amazing relationship?

You've already taken the first step to making it happen – you've purchased this book because you are ready!

This book will guide you to accomplishing goals using the S.M.A.R.T. System and other powerful strategies to keep motivated and focused until you achieve your goal.

In the following Chapters, there will be 10 core steps to start strong, and reach the finish line at full speed thinking, "Wow that was fun and easier than I thought!"

At the end of each Chapter, there will be a simple and fun task for you to complete to bring you closer to accomplishing your goal.

This book for both people who need that extra push to get it completed, and for people who do not know 100% what they want or how to get it.

You will soon be staying motivated, focused, and *building* your life instead of sitting back and watching life pass you by!

Let's begin!

Chapter 1: What are SMART Goals?

The S.M.A.R.T. System is a way to accomplish tasks faster and easier and majorly increase your productivity. Successful CEO's, entrepreneurs, brainiacs, and people like you and me use the SMART system to achieve our goals. It is the backbone to success. I've read books and emulated people who have been successful in life such as Richard Branson, Oprah Winfrey, and Steve Jobs. They all have one thing in common- they set create SMART Goals, get into action and along the way use strategies to keep the dream alive until it is achieved.

For example Richard Branson's vision of creating the Virgin Galactic which can launch you to outer space; or Oprah Winfrey's vision of creating the Leadership Foundation Academy which is a free school for young girls in South Africa; and of course Steve Jobs who envisioned creating the Apple iPhone, iPad, and Apple HDTV were all dreams that became realities.

This system is rooted on the sole principle that: Life does not control us, instead we are in control of our lives.

The good news is that this system can be used to complete almost any task. It takes a complicated process and breaks it down into simple, manageable pieces that line up like ducks in a row.

Welcome to the S.M.A.R.T. System, which stands for: Specific, Measurable, Attainable, Realistic, and

Timeline. Here's an example I used to successfully start a coaching business:

- **Specific:** I will launch a life coaching business.

- **Measurable:** I will be sign up my first paying client within 2 weeks, and give a one sample coaching session a day (5 per week).

- **Attainable:** I will attend one networking event each day. There I will meet the speaker and two other people, and get their contact information. I will follow up with these people the following day and offer them a sample coaching session. After each session I will find out if they want to continue coaching with me and offer them specific value they will receive from coaching with me.

- **Relevant:** Coaching people will allow me to make a positive impact in other peoples' lives and lead them to answers, which I am very passionate about.

- **Timeline:** Roots Coaching will have its first paying client in two weeks. By December 31, I will have 10 coaching clients.

Jump In The SMART Way

As mentioned before, the S.M.A.R.T. System is an acronym that stands for Specific, Measurable, Attainable, Realistic, and Timely. ALL five components are essential to success with the S.M.A.R.T system; failing to complete even one step will significantly reduce the chances of success. If you leave one out, it would be like building a table, but forgetting to attach one of the legs.

One of the most rewarding things about having goals is that you will wake up feeling more excited about your day, knowing that the days of your life are filled with a specific purpose.

Lets first take a look at some examples of how to utilize the S.M.A.R.T system with regard to career, health, and relationships.

Health

The gym is always flooded in January with people who have New Year Resolutions to lose 5, 10, 20 pounds or get 6-pack abs. Then it begins to dwindle down month by month. This is because people either don't have a compelling enough reason to continue working-out and lose motivation, or they get too busy and the Resolution is soon forgotten about until next January.

You can use S.M.A.R.T. to stay on track and keep moving forward with your exercise regime and eating habits in order to lose weight and/or gain muscle. It can help you to find out if the regime you have chosen is working for you by applying the "Specific" and "Measurable" components.

For example, you could say "I will lose between 1.5-2 pounds each week for six weeks, and then after a week goes by you can look at your progress and see if you've lost 1.5-2lbs each week. If not, go back through your week and determine what you can cut out to improve *this* week – maybe cut out the late night junk food snacks, or go to the gym 4 times instead of twice. This is also where a Health journal can come handy for tracking the food you ate and exercise completed.

Love

The S.M.A.R.T rule can also be used in your love life. Finding love is important to all of us. To find love, you need to have a solid plan to finding the person that you will love in life. In other words, it is ideal to create qualities that a potential love partner needs to have to be compatible. Be Specific about the top 3 qualities you want your love partner to have.

For example you could say, "Connection, Adventure, and Intelligence;" or "Funny, Charming, and Romantic." Then as you meet people, learn about them and decide if that person has the top 3 qualities you're looking for. You can also do this for the top 3 qualities you CAN NOT have. For example, "Negative,

Loud, or Extremely Jealous", or whatever qualities you don't like.

Then think about activities you enjoy doing, for example if it's hiking you could join a hiking club or hiking meetup group on Also, think of what your Timeline when it comes to dating – for example, "I will have a girlfriend by March 1st (2-months away) and I will meet two new women 5 days a week."

Often love is not planned, and it is not known when Mr. or Miss Right will appear, but having a plan in place will increase chances for success when you see someone that looks like a potential partner. So, if this is what you want create a plan, get into action and make it happen.

With the SMART planning process, you will be able to find someone you love faster while keeping yourself from wasting time on people you aren't likely to have a happy relationship, minimizing the likelihood of encountering disappointments. The key is to be as specific as you can when it comes to finding someone to love.

Happiness

Finally, you can use this rule in order to increase happiness; for some, happiness is created from external factors such as: a financial reward, or acquiring a beautiful home. Others get happiness from learning a new talent, or taking a vacation or moving to a new city and feeling at peace while listening to the waves crash against the rocks. Some want to have a luxury car while others want to invent something. Writers want to create the perfect book while athletes want to be stronger and more efficient in their respective sports. If one of the ideas mentioned here is resonating for you, keep that in mind and apply it in the next chapter.

Another note on happiness is that it is really easy to access, much easier than people make it out to be. It involves being in the present moment, and enjoying *every* moment. You may be thinking how is that possible? That is not the topic of this book, and if you'd like more details, I highly recommend my book titled, where I go into detail and provide steps to achieving inner peace and happiness.

Step 1:

Before you start planning for your future, there are certain things that you need to establish. First, give yourself some time today to assess your life. Grab a piece of paper, and go to a quiet spot in your home. Now, sit down in that quiet place, take a few deep breaths as you relax.

Take a look at the following categories and rank them 1-10 with 1 meaning 'nonexistent',

and 10 being 'the best!' Go ahead and rank your life today.

1. Family and Friends

2. Health

3. Money

4. Career

5. Fun and Recreation

6. Significant Other/Romance

7. Physical Location

8. Personal Growth

Look back over the categories. What do you want to change in each of these categories? What do you need to do to bring you closer to a 10? Take a second and imagine being there. What would it look like? (You can say it aloud to yourself – I won't tell.)

- Imagine your life if NOTHING changed, and it stayed at the same level 1 month from now, 6 months, and one year from now.
- How bad do you want this life you're imagining?
- Imagine tomorrow. What do you see?

Now that you have your list of areas that are strong and areas that you want to improve, you can use these ratings as a starting points and work to improve them. This will allow you to check in every so often (i.e. weekly, monthly, etc.) to see where improvements have been made. Let's keep moving forward!

Chapter 2: How to Set An Unbreakable SMART Goal!

WHY do you want to achieve your goal? What will it bring you? You must answer this question or stop reading. This answer will be one of your strongest motivators.

S is for SPECIFIC

Your goal must be specific. The more specific your goal is, the greater chance at successfully accomplishing it. Take for example "I want to lose weight". But I say, "Ok that's great! How much do you want to lose?"

"I want to lose 15 pounds." Clearly this is more specific.

Here are a few more examples of specific goals:

- I will earn a $100,000 per year in my online business.
- I will drive a brand new Mercedes S Class.
- I will buy a new house.
- I will lose 15 pounds.
- I will be in a fun, healthy relationship with a person I connect with, can have deep conversations with, and who is adventurous.

Make It Observable

To ensure that your plan is specific, make it observable. Make it so that you can hear or see yourself doing it. A person should be able to see it. For example you should see or imagine yourself driving a brand new Mercedes S Class, or see yourself walking into your new house, or see the $100,000 on your bank statement, etc.

The Roadmap

Of course, creating a plan to reach this goal is important. It's like a roadmap to your destination. You must start from point A and get to point B, but in between there could be traffic, detours, or stops that need to be made along the way. With a plan, you can organize all the necessary actions and establish a schedule for when things need to be accomplished to stay on track.

Otherwise, if you're always in the dark and you do not have a plan, you will surely not be able to get your goal by anything other than luck or chance, or you may achieve it but you might not even realize it.

With specific plans, every idea used will have a specified task. For example if you want to make $1,000 more per month, make a list of things you need to accomplish to get there. If you're in sales, maybe you need to contact 15 new prospects per day instead of the usual 10. Maybe you need to set up 10 appointments per week instead of 8. Make out a schedule and set up specific times you will do this. For example on MWF, I will make calls from 1-5pm, with two 20 minute breaks; and on Tuesday and Thursday I will have appointments to meet with 5 people between 11am and 7pm. Again, it goes back to being as specific as possible.

Another example could be if your goal were to lose 10 pounds, you could say, "To feel more attractive I will lose 10 pounds in 3 months by joining a gym and working out MWF from 12pm-1pm", and so forth.

Language

Another key point is to use language that appeals to you because the language can significantly change how you feel about your goal. Words produce emotion. They can excite you, or make you feel nothing at all. The objective should be to make the language as exciting and compelling as possible.

Here's an example, "I will easily drop 10 pounds of fat to feel more attractive, weighing 150 pounds at 13% body fat, while totally loving the process." Others things you can use might be, "To have a sexy body," or "To have more energy," – whatever works for you so that you can feel energized and excited about your goal.

Step 2: Make Your Goal Specific. Look at the examples above, and make your goal specific enough so anyone can be clear on what it is *you want*. For example, "To bring out my

creative side and make an income, I will launch a start a Photography Business."

M is for Measurable

The task of measuring something may seem super simple and easy, although it is usually the task people have the most difficulty with. So, if you don't measure it how can you know when your goal is EVER met; and how can you make any changes if you make a mistake so that you do not keep going in circles?

Your goal needs to be something you can measure on a regular basis. Most people set their New Year Resolutions, but fail to look at the progress or regression, leaving them incomplete and eventually forgotten. Another reason the goals need to be specific is because you can't measure "I want to earn more money", but you can measure "I want to make $1000 each week."

A measurable goal shows tangible evidence for any progress or regression. It can be used as an indicator that the goal has been achieved. Your goal must be something that you can measure regularly (e.g. weekly, bi-weekly). It is important to track progress and decide which, if any changes need to be made.

Put it on your calendar, or set an alarm so that whenever it goes off you have to stop everything and take your measurements to see your progress. To maximize this process, you must have a way of measuring the goal consistently to see whether or not you're making progress. A weekly check-in or review is usually sufficient for goals to determine what is working or if anything needs to be changed. You can't measure, "I want to lose weight", but you can measure "I want to lose 15 pounds in 6 months."

We need to measure to our progress to see results. It is hard to see changes from day to day because you are with yourself all day long. It's kind of like when you start working out for a few weeks and you don't feel like you look any different, then a friend says to you, "Have you been working out? You're looking good." You may have not noticed, but your friend did – that's the role that tracking your progress will play.

When you're seeing positive results you'll be more motivated to keep working hard. Measuring your plans will let you know exactly when you have accomplished your goals, and then you can celebrate or reward yourself for your achievement.

Step 3:

Make Your SMART Goal *Measurable*: If you have, "I will lose 15 pounds." When will you have it completed by? Can you break it down further? For example if you have "I will lose 15 pounds in 4 months," you could say, "Each week for the next six months I will lose 1 pound per week and will happily go to the gym

three times a week (treadmill 20 min, and lift weights 30 minutes).

A is for Attainable

Your goal must be attainable. If you set up a goal that is impossible to attain, then you are setting yourself up for failure and will likely be disappointed in yourself. So let's make it attainable.

You can attain almost any goal you set when you plan your steps wisely, establish a time frame that allows you to perform those steps, and make the goal compelling enough that it MUST get done.

Step 4: Make Your SMART Goal Attainable

A coach of mine taught me an easy and fun way to discover attainable goals. Here's what she recommended. First, take out a pen and paper and create a list of words that you believe about yourself including your current skills and strengths. If this isn't easy to do, then you can ask a family member or a friend to name a few of your recognizable positive qualities.

Next take a look at your goal and match your qualities you'll need to bring to the table to reach your goal. You can base 'what is

Attainable' on your past achievements, such as any awards you were given or milestones at work.

Then think of the qualities you have that will contribute to the process of the goal. For example, you could say, "Charm, Education, and People/Social Skills". Keep that paper as a reminder of what skills you have and as something you can look at if you begin to doubt yourself or lose hope in your goal.

GOAL:

_____

_____

My Qualities that will contribute to achieving this:

1.

_____

—

2.

_____

—

3.

_____

—

4.

_____

—

5.

R is for Realistic

Your goal must be realistic. How realistic are your plans? Are you planning to make $1,000,000 by next year? Or lose 5 pounds in a week? Or buy a $500,000 house if your income is only $40,000 per year. All of these are *possible*, but sometimes the hardest question is - Are the realistic?

If you want to earn $100,000 next month, but you don't have a job, that is not realistic. I encourage thinking big. However, if you set a goal that is too unrealistic so that even YOU don't believe that it can happen, it can have damaging effects, such as continuously letting yourself down. Instead of feeling gratified and accomplished, you could end up feeling worse about yourself than before.

In most cases, realistic plans will be tangible. You should be able to experience it through your senses including: taste, smell, sight, touch and auditory.

Considerations

Dreams you have right now may be realistic if you work hard, plan ahead, and keep pushing even when the times get tough. However, some of your dreams may not be financially possible at the moment, so make a plan to make it financially possible, if you want it bad enough – and set up a savings plan so you can save money towards it. Before you dive in to this goal, you must break it down and determine if that goal will work for you.

If your goal is to have the perfect abs, you should set the right timeline so that your goal will be attainable. If you need more information on figuring out a realistic timeline, there are many health magazines that can guide you, or you can hire a personal trainer to show you strategies to reach your health goal.

The Attainable and Realistic Rules complement each other. If your dreams are not attainable then they might not be realistic. The point is that there are some things that can be realistic to some people and not to others. Be honest with yourself when considering if your goal is realistic.

For instance, if your goal is to spend more time with the family instead of work so much, you are going to have to say "no" to a lot more things to make the "family time". If you know that you are not willing to (or cannot spend less time at work), then it is not a realistic goal, unless you are willing to make other sacrifices (such as less sleep, or less extra-curricular activities) to have more balance between work and family time.

If you need help deciding whether it's possible or not, consider asking a close friend or family member. Also, I recommend not asking anyone who is pessimistic by nature because they will likely shut you're goal down completely. So go ask a trustworthy, neutral to optimistic minded person.

Step 5: Make Your SMART Goal Realistic

<u>**Answer these Questions:**</u>

- **Does it fit in your lifestyle?**
- **Do you have enough time to spend each week to make it a success?**
- **Do you have the financial means to begin?**
- **Do you have the knowledge or skills?**
- **Do you have the passion and perseverance to do what it takes to accomplish this?**

If the answer is "No" to these questions, then it's important to either modify, or reconsider your goal.

T is For Timeline

For a goal to be complete, it needs to be timely or have a timeline. A goal should be supported within a time frame. If there is no time frame, then there will no sense of urgency. If you want to lose 10 lbs., when do you want to lose it by? "Someday" won't work. But if you place it within a timeframe, "by May 1st", then you've set your unconscious mind into motion to begin working on the goal.

Will you have a wall calendar, or a flipbook calendar to mark your progress and remind yourself of deadlines? How about sticky notes all over your office or bedroom?

If your plan is based on a 10 to 20 year process, then you might have a hard time keeping your goal in mind and it will likely shift (which is okay). However, over time it might be difficult to keep pushing forward because it is so far out in the distance.

The solution to distant goals is to break them down into smaller pieces. Meaning that if you have a goal to have 5 million dollars in your bank account in 10 years, then it needs to be broken down into smaller parts (e.g. a 5 year plan, a 1 year plan, 1 month plan, and so forth). Goals that are smaller such as 1 week, 1 month, or even 1 year are much easier to see than 10 years down the road.

Make It Urgent

Think about the power of a deadline. For instance, when you were in school there was pressure to complete an assignment or else there would be consequences – maybe after-school detention or a failing grade, requiring you to retake the course or even get expelled.

You want to create pressure on yourself to get it done. Create urgency.

Having consequences for not achieving a goal can be a strong motivator to get over the hurdles.

For example, if you don't complete your goal by your set deadline, what will you do that causes a bit of a sting? Will you give $500 to your neighbor or a charity or a homeless man on the street? If you commit to this for each of your goals, imagine how many goals you will accomplish!

Step 6: Give Your SMART Goal a Timeline and make it Urgent!

What is a realistic timeline you can commit to for achieving your SMART Goal? Add a deadline (and urgency) to your goal, such as, "I will lose 15 pounds in 4 months (by July 31). If I do not, then I must donate $100 to a stranger behind me in Starbucks on (fill in a date).

Chapter 3: Why You(and everyone else in the world) Needs SMART Goals!

Life can be chaotic, messy, and stressful. We can't deny that. Some days you may wake up thinking of all the things you need to accomplish today and thinking there is NO WAY you can possibly get all of it done! Stress is created and the important part is how you *choose* to use it.

Do you use it to energize yourself and get you going, accomplishing tasks at a more rapid pace than usual?

Or do you use the stress as a reason to mope, feel sorry for yourself, and stay in bed, getting very little accomplished? If you feel this way, here is a helpful strategy.

It is a perspective shift strategy, answering the following questions:

- *Who is someone you admire?*
  - o *Examples could be a loved one (mom or dad), Richard Branson, Tony Robbins*

- *If that person were looking at you right now, what would he/she say for you to do?*

- *Use this as inspiration and motivation to get up and get busy!*

If you'd like to learn more about perspective shifts and ways to have a mindset so that you can attract what you want into your life, I highly recommend my book on Neurolinguistic Programming.

Habits

If your life is not the way you want it, it will stay that way until you consciously make the effort to change. Once you decide *what* you want, take small steps each day for 30 days until it becomes a habit and feels natural. For example, if you have a goal to lower your body fat%, you may have a plan to go to the gym every M,W,F, and walk 2 miles on your off days. If you do this for 30 days, it'll become a habit. In fact, if you did this for 30 days, it'd feel strange if you didn't work out on those days, especially if you're seeing results – similar to the way it feels like when you don't brush your teeth one night (or morning).

Other examples might include writing a book for 1 hour a day (which is how I wrote this book), or working on your business for an hour a day, or going to a coffee shop to meet 2 new people for an hour a day in order to network or find a new relationship – doing each for 30 days to form a habit.

Comfort Zone

One of the hardest parts to reaching a goal is not only changing old habits, but also stepping outside of your comfort zone. Your comfort zone is where you feel most comfortable, but it brings only minimal rewards.

Getting outside of your comfort zone is where you will find massive growth and reach your goals. It's fascinating to see what happens if you get uncomfortable and find out what your capable of achieving.

For example, when I finally gained the courage to talk to people who I thought were intimidating – for example...the beautiful woman, the stiff professional, our wealthy intimidating boss. Once I shifted my perspective using NLP, my life had completely changed – these people were on the same level as me and now I felt comfortable and encouraged to talk with them.

After practicing shifting my perspectives with NLP techniques, I'd gotten my introverted self to be comfortable talking to anyone. After using these NLP strategies for several months, I saw a gorgeous girl sitting on a bench, and I had the courage and confidence to talk with her – the whole time thinking "OMG, this girl is WAY out of my league, and she's talking to me!" Then I got to know who she really was, and she had become the most beautiful girl I'd ever met.

Ultimately it is fear that is our worst enemy. What are you afraid of? Fear keeps people in the comfort zone, never attempting to reach for their goals. I know this because I did it for years. I was afraid of rejection;

afraid of talking to people I'd never met and would probably never see again.

I encourage you to see what happens if you talk to that person in the coffee shop, or apply to that lucrative job, or take the leap to start a business that you're passionate about. If it doesn't work the first time, do it again, and maybe again until it happens. You'll notice that each time you do it, it becomes easier and more fun!

Managing Your Life

One of the most challenging parts to goal setting is finding the time to work toward it. Most likely, you are already extremely busy. That means you will have to say 'no' to a few more things or cut back on something else in your life.

Think about the things you spend time on that you really aren't necessary – Facebook, Instagram, Twitter, Phone, Texting, TV, You Tube. If you cut back 1 hour per day and took that hour to chase your goals, imagine where you would be in one month or one year.

24 hours, 60 minutes in 1 hour

Each of us is given the same amount of hours and minutes each day. The most significant factor separating people who win at goal setting and people who lose is how you spend your time.

- How do you spend your time?
  Be curious about how and where your time is spent. Track it for a week. It is a good way for you to find out what you truly value in life.

Life is not about waiting for the right time to come. It's about doing all the right things in the time that is given to you.

Your Life Is Your Creation

It is important to understand that everything you've created in your life right now is something that you've set forth to get. Your life isn't an accident. You've focused your energy on something over a period of time and the things in your life were created - both the things you DO and DON'T want in your life. You must accept responsibility for *your* actions, which is one of the first steps to transforming your life.

You've created and manifested the job you love or hate, the amazing or awful relationship you're in, and the financial freedom or endless debt. You created it. The point is that if you can think it and believe it it, then you can create it. The other point being that you and ONLY you can change your circumstances. *You* can change your mindset, pre-existing beliefs, or perspective for literally *any* situation.

As Rhonda Byrnes said in her widely recognized book The Secret, "Thoughts become things." Whatever you focus your energy and attention on will manifest in your life. This is one of the reasons it is so important to keep a positive mindset and use positive language.

It sometimes takes a boatload of effort to see the glass half full -especially when things haven't been going the way you want. But, when you think about it, there is always something positive or good that can be uncovered in every situation, and that is where your energy should be focused instead of on everything that went wrong.

I'm not saying to completely ignore the negative things, but instead don't worry or dwell on the 'what if's' because you can't change the past, you can only learn from your experiences so you can do better next time.

Step 7: Get a calendar in order for you to schedule and commit to your goal. For example, from 6-8pm MWF, I will completely commit to meeting new people to network with (or begin a relationship with) – nothing else; or from 7-8am M-F I will work on the new business I am creating.

Mark each day up until your goal on your Timeline. For example, if you want your goal completed in 3 months, I recommend blocking out the times each day and marking what you need to do for each of those days for you to reach to your goal.

Chapter 4: Staying Fired Up About Your Goals!

Motivation and drive are necessary to complete a task. The reality is that every action is driven by motivation. You get up from the couch to get a glass of water to quench your thirst; you read this book because you're motivated to learn something new or get more information or to get motivated to achieving goals.

One of the strongest motivators for the human race is wealth in order to provide for yourself and your family, as well as buy the car or house you desire. Others are motivated by personal achievements, such as Roger Banister in 1954 who dreamed of crushing the 4-min mile.

The S.M.A.R.T System in itself is also a form of motivation since you have discovered and answered all the questions in the previous chapters. Review your answers to these questions on a regular basis – some prefer daily and others review it every two weeks to keep focused and motivated; some read it multiple times a day to keep up the momentum, or when they are feeling discouraged or want a reminder of why they are shooting for this goal in the first place. Figure out what works best for you and make it a routine or ritual to review it regularly.

Take care of yourself

One of the simplest, yet most forgotten or overlooked things when it comes to maximizing your chances of success...is the importance of taking care of the goal maker - yourself. This is especially important if you are under additional stress.

A few quick notes are to:

> **Remember to breathe-** take a few deep breaths at least every hour to get more oxygen to your cells - it will help you feel better and more relaxed.

> **Keep hydrated** by drinking at least 6-8 cups of water each day

> **Keep healthy snacks around** – raisins, carrots, celery sticks, pistachios, etc.

> **Get up and move around at least once an hour** to get your blood flowing throughout your body

> **Make time in your schedule for a recharge** – 20 min nap, meditation, or walk

Perseverance

Michael Jordan, one of the most celebrated athletes in the world, knows all about perseverance. When Jordan was a sophomore in high school, he failed to make the basketball team. The coaches said he was too short to play basketball being only 5'11 (1.80m).

Instead of giving up or feeling down about being "too short" and not making the basketball team, he turned it around and made it positive. Michael Jordan stated, "Whenever I was working out and got tired and figured I ought to stop, I'd close my eyes and see that list in the locker room without my name on it and that usually got me going again."

Jordan didn't make excuses. His dream was to be the best on the court. With strong perseverance and refusal to quit, he practiced more than his peers, which led him to becoming one of the greatest basketball players of all time.

Grit

Psychologist Angela Lee Duckworth conducted an extensive research study and found that the highest predictor of a person's success is "grit" - the combination of "perseverance and passion for long-term goals." The willingness to fail and keep moving forward is what sets successful people apart from the rest.

Thomas Edison made over 1,000 light bulbs before inventing one that finally worked.

Walt Disney was fired from a newspaper company because the editor said he "lacked imagination and had no good ideas".

Albert Einstein didn't speak until age four and didn't read until age seven. His teachers labeled him "slow" and "mentally handicapped." But Einstein just had a different way of thinking. He later won the Nobel Prize in Physics.

Dr. Seuss' first book was thrown out by 27 different publishers before finally getting published. He's now the most popular children's book author ever.

The reason these people made it was because they kept pushing forward even when the tide was pushing against them. The point being that it is okay to fail. Just because you fail many times doesn't mean you're a failure. It just means that you've learned ways that do not work for you.

Self-Image

Our self-image controls our lives more than anything else. You are what you think you are. If you don't see yourself being successful, you won't. You can't be it if you can't see it. Your life is limited to your vision. If you want to change your life, you must first change your vision of your life.

A well-known figure of someone who envisioned himself becoming the #1 paid movie star in Hollywood is a man by the name of Arnold Schwarzenegger. He was unknown to most people in 1976 when a newspaper reporter asked him, "Now that you've retired from bodybuilding, what do you plan to do next?" He answered very calmly and confidently, "I'm going to be the #1 movie star in Hollywood."

The reporter was shocked and amused by Schwarzenegger's response. It was hard to believe that a huge bodybuilder, who had no experience acting and spoke poor English with a strong Austrian accent, could ever be the #1 movie star in Hollywood!

The reporter asked him how he planned to make this dream come true, and Schwarzenegger stated, "I'll do it the same way I became the #1 body builder in the world. I first create a vision of who I want to be, then I start living like that person in my mind as if it were already true." That sounds almost too childish and too simple to be true, doesn't it? But, it worked! Years later Schwarzenegger became the highest paid movie star in Hollywood.

Take Schwarzenegger as an inspiration (or anyone you look up to) and think, "If he (or she) can do it, I CAN TOO...AND I WILL."

Confidence Builders:

Self-confidence can play a role.

If you want to boost your confidence, here are some things you can do:

1. Start doing positive affirmations **every morning** before you start your day. Positive affirmations are telling yourself both who you want to be and reminding yourself of the amazing qualities you already have – and the key word is **positive**, so keep all the words positive.

For example, you might want to read off a list or look in the mirror and say aloud, "I am confident in myself. I am optimistic. I am intelligent. People admire me, etc." Don't just say it, but really feel it and believe it. I remember when I first started this, I felt ridiculous, and after a week or so it became normal routine and I could feel and feel my self-limiting beliefs begin to fade.

It has powerful effects on your subconscious and soon you'll be the person you want to be. Now create the list of qualities you want to have.

2. Surround yourself around people who already have high confidence and model their behavior. Often times the best way to learn is to

observe and then imitate people. It's kind of like when your playing a sport - although it may be intimidating, it is far better for you to play with people who are better than you because your learning curve will significantly increase.

Step 8: Take a realistic view of yourself - Do you need to improve one of these qualities. If so, take some time to improve it. For instance, if you want to feel more confident, do positive affirmations for a few weeks. If you're satisfied where you are at, let's move forward.

Chapter 5: The Master Plan To SMART Goals

These are the most important questions to ask whenever setting a Goal. Also, I've included a few of my personal goals from 2013. You can use my examples as starting points, guidelines, or however is most helpful for you.

To set a S.M.A.R.T. goal, answer these 10 questions:

*Why do you want this Goal?

1. What is something you want to accomplish?

2. What is important about this?

3. Who will be involved in completing the task?

4. When will you start?

5. Where will it happen?

6. What are the requirements and constraints?

7. What are the action steps I need to take to get it done?

8. Why do I need to accomplish this certain task?

9. When do you want it completed?

10. What are the consequences of not completing it?

*Why do you want this goal? (Yes again. Answer and solidify the answer.)

Once you have the answered all these questions, your goal will be specific and you will be on track for it to be a S.M.A.R.T. and highly effective plan.

Here's an example: "I will lose 15 pounds by going to the gym for 1 hour every M, W, F, and Sun. At the gym, I'll do 30 minutes cardio and the other 30 strength-training. Once every 2 weeks, I will check in to see the progress made and to see if any adjustments need to be made. If I do this then I will feel better about myself, have more energy. If I do not do this, I will give $20 to my parents for each day I miss." And Bam! That's it! That's a S.M.A.R.T. goal.

Here are a few examples of my goals that I posted on a bulletin board in my bedroom and office. I'd read them every morning before I started my day to remind myself of my S.M.A.R.T. goals and how important it is for me to achieve them.

1. I will easily have a thriving life-coaching business by 12.31.13 (15 clients, $----/session)

Why?

- To make an income so I can travel the world, eat where I want, and create a family someday!

- To not have to struggle and worry about how I will survive

- To show others that I CAN do it!

- If I don't achieve it, I will have to find a shitty job that I don't like just to make money to survive!

How?

- Have fun at Networking Events, Lead Networking Events & Give Speeches On: Goals, Positivity, Dating Coaching, and Being In The Present Moment

*If I achieve this goal, I will go on a fun, relaxing vacation in Cabo for NYE.

*If I don't do this, I will donate $100 to a charity of my choice.

2. I will easily be part of the (_____ improvisation organization by 12.31.13

Why?

- To be admired and looked up to by my peers

- To meet and form relationships with people I admire

- To have better social skills

- I love learning about people

How?

- Interview by 7.31.14, Display Learned Skills, Share knowledge with Students

*If I don't do this, I will never be able to make money with all the hours I've spent practicing improv.

*When I achieve this goal, I will go on a $500 shopping spree.

*If I don't do this, I will donate $100 to a charity of my choice

3. I will easily Create an Impressive Introduction 'Life Coach' Video 7.15.13

Why?

- I will impress myself, my friends, and family and they can promote me too because it will be awesome!

- To show potential clients "in person" who they would be talking to, making them more comfortable and more likely to want to connect with me

How?

- Make Script by 7.9.14, Film Video by 7.15.14

* If I don't do this, I won't be taking my business to the next level, and will always be making less money than I could have.

* When I achieve this goal, I will go to the movie theatre!

* If I don't do this, I will donate $100 to a charity of my choice

4. I will easily have a fit, toned, attractive body by 9.30.13

Why?

- Because I don't want back pain

- Because I like to look toned and fit

- It shows others that I respect myself me because I take care of my body

- I will fit better in my clothes- making me look better

How?

- Lift weights 3-5 X/week, cardio 30 min

* If I don't do this, my back will hurt and I won't be as confident about my appearance

* When I achieve this goal, I will sign up for a surfing lesson.

* If I don't do this, I will donate $100 to a charity of my choice

Step 9: First, answer the 10 questions above and write your answers down, then keep it as a reminder of how you originally felt about your SMART goal(you'll find out why in the next chapter).

Chapter 6: Final Secrets That Only Few Know!

- **A goal-board (vision board) has proven to be very effective strategies to making dreams reality.** It is simply a large bulletin board that has pictures of things people want to achieve in life – such as financial freedom, or a dream home, or dream car; what is included on it to make it a goal board is the numbers (such as the income you want to earn this month or this year), and specific steps you can read each morning before you start your day to make progress toward your goal.

Visualization is important when it comes to dreaming and reaching goals. It is an exhilarating feeling to relish the joy of seeing your back account with a five million dollar balance. It gives you the energy and will power to work diligently toward your goal.

The more you desire something, the more effort you'll put into reaching your goal. The more you visualize that your dream can come true, the more inspired you'll be to make it happen.

When it comes to goal setting, the mind and the body are most effective when they can work synergistically. The more you want it and the more clear you can see it in your mind, the more your body is energized and wants to go out and do what the mind is envisioning.

- **Fake It Until You Make It**
  I don't like to say you have to lie to yourself...but in reality you do – you have to act like you've already achieved your goal, and not just *act* like it, but actually *believe* it. Believe you already have gotten a raise so that you can actually feel what it feels like to receive the raise. Remember *that feeling* and how to access it because you can use that as a simple way to motivate you if you're feeling unmotivated.

- **Put a large dry-erase board on your wall or even several walls**. List your goals on it. Next to or below each goal, would be a list of the tasks and the days they need to be completed by - and of course after it's completed, you can put a sweet little checkmark.

Once you put up the board, look at it every morning when you wake up and every evening before you go to sleep. This will allow you to constantly keep your goal toward the front of your mind. It's also a good reminder of how much progress you've made.

- **If you want something bad enough, think about it, and keep thinking about it**

multiple times throughout your day.
Again, this is because you're thoughts influence your actions, so the more you think about your goal, the more likely your actions will be synchronous with your thoughts.

One of the most powerful motivational stories was the story of Anthony Burgess who's best known for *A Clockwork Orange.* He had a brain tumor and was told he would die within a year. He knew he had a battle on his hands. He barely had enough money to feed his family, and had nothing to leave behind for his wife, Lynne, soon to be a widow.

Burgess was never been a professional novelist in the past, but he *always had thoughts of becoming a writer.* Since he'd been diagnosed with a brain tumor, these thought of ways to make money through writing books were constantly on his mind. He was determined to leave something behind so he pursued writing. He did not have a clue whether or not his book would get published, but he still went for it, with the primary purpose of leaving money behind for his wife.

He stated, "It was January of 1960, and according to the prognosis, I had a winter and spring and summer to live through, and would die with the fall of the leaf."

During that time Burgess wrote energetically, finishing five and a half novels by the time the year was over. But, Burgess did not die. His cancer had gone into remission and then completely disappeared. In his long and full life as an author, he wrote over 70 books. Without the death sentence of one year, he may not have written at all.

Many of us are like Anthony Burgess, hiding our brilliance inside. If you only had one year to live, how would you live differently? What would you do?

- **If you are beginning to lose steam with your goal, remember the big picture.** Remember those 10 questions you answered in Chapter 5? Take a look at those and the answers.

For example, when I was getting my college degree I was required to take some courses I – for the lack of a better term, could not stand because the subject matter was so boring to me, and it was much harder to get thing to click. It felt like going for a goal *without a purpose*, until I recalled the big picture – getting a college degree, which will allow me to have a job, which will allow me to have a house, where I would be able to raise a family).

So, the way to persevere when you are losing momentum is to constantly remind yourself of the big picture. "Ultimately, this _(fill in the blank)_ will get me to (_this goal_)." You can even add this to your vision board (or picture on your desk; or as your screen saver) if you want a silent reminder of your goal.

- **Positive Affirmations**

I touched on this in Chapter 4. They are both confidence builders as well as very strong ways to stay motivated. They will allow yourself to become "your ideal self". I strongly suggest adding these to your daily routines to maximize your goal success. Review these in Chapter 4 to get started, if you haven't already.

- **Powerful Questions**

Answer these questions and write your answers down:

1. What is important about this goal?

2. How will my life be different after I achieve this?

3. How will I feel once it is accomplished?

4. What will I miss out on if I don't accomplish my goal?

5. How will I feel if I don't pursue my goal?

Use your answers as a reminder for why you *need* to accomplish your goal.

- ## The Power of Positivity, the Mind & Success
  The mindset has a lot to do with how successful you'll be. You've probably heard someone say, "Be more positive", or "You're so negative!"

Which one stings a more? "You're so negative!" does, although essentially the same thing. The difference is that one has a positive spin on it and the other is negative. If you swap the negative words in your vocabulary with positive ones, your subconscious mind will pick up on it, and you will begin to see things in a more positive light.

If you aren't already doing this, try it for at least 3 weeks. First mark down how you feel overall, and in 3 weeks let me know how you feel. You can email me:. And for some accountability, each time you use a negative word, put a $1 in a bucket. Then at the end of 3 weeks, donate the money to a charity of your choice. Or take on any other accountability technique that causes a little bit of a bite or sting.

I go into much more detail in my _Positivity_ book, which reveals strategies to have keep positive mindset and attract what you want into your life.

- **Accountability**

Holding yourself accountable, or having someone such as a friend, family member, or even hiring a life coach to hold you accountable to your commitment is one of the most important components of achieving any goal. The example above of putting $1 in a bucket is an example of self accountability; if you hired a coach, he or she could send you text reminders, calls or whatever works best for you to get what you need accomplished.

You can also create a "contract" in order to hold yourself accountable. Be sure to make it SMART and list the penalties if you do not abide by the terms. Give it to a friend to make sure you abide by it, and be sure to sign it as well.

I promise myself to maximize my effort to achieve the following goals by the listed deadline:

1.

_____

_____

_____by _____

2.

_____

_____

_____by _____

- **Reward Yourself**

Once your achieve your goal, no matter how big or small, be sure to reward yourself. Maybe your goal is to eat healthy six days of the week. If you do that, then reward yourself with your favorite meal on the 7th day of the week. Maybe you have a goal of building a business, which might take years to build. When you accomplish that go out and do something fun or buy a car, or an extravagant vacation. The point is to be sure to reward yourself for all the work you put in, for every milestone. Begin rewarding yourself by taking a moment to feel proud of yourself for reading this book.

Adjust When Needed

Remember that revising plans is a good thing. Be able to roll with the punches and when something doesn't go as planned be willing to adjust. There will always be unforeseen bumps in the road. Those little bumps on the road will inevitably be there and they will often put a dent in your plans. If you're feeling discouraged, go back and read your goals, and why you need to accomplish them, or spend some time viewing your vision board and feel how amazing it would feel to have it accomplished.

Step 10: Commit to at least 3 of these motivators to keep yourself feeling strong about yourself and your goal until it is accomplished. Now, go make it happen!

Conclusion

Remember that your dreams will only become a reality if you are determined enough to step outside of your comfort zone and challenge your self-limiting beliefs in order to create the life you desire.

I've learned over the past 5 years that whatever goal you might have, whatever you can dream of, you can achieve. There are no limits unless you put them on yourself.

Of course it does not come at the drop of a hat or from complete luck, but instead with perseverance and commitment.

I hope this book was helpful and got you clear on how to reach your goals.

I wish you the best with your future goals and dreams.

Made in the USA
Lexington, KY
17 May 2018